HILARY *and* JACKIE

Cello Album

Music *by* Edward Elgar &
Barrington Pheloung

Collection *of* music
from the film
for cello & piano

Novello

Exclusive distributors:
Music Sales Limited
Newmarket Road, Bury St Edmunds, Suffolk IP33 3YB
All rights reserved.

Order No. NOV120857
ISBN 0-85360-960-8
This book © Copyright 1999 Novello & Company Limited.
14–15 Berners Street, London W1T 3LJ

Cover design by Michael Bell Design Limited.

CONTENTS

CELLO CONCERTO

1st movement (Adagio, Moderato)

Edward Elgar
Arranged by the composer
for cello and piano

6

10

THE HOLIDAY SONG

Based on a theme by Bernard Fleiss

Barrington Pheloung

THE FARMHOUSE

Barrington Pheloung

SISTERS

Barrington Pheloung

Collection *of* music
from the film
for cello & piano

HILARY *and* JACKIE

Cello Album

Music *by* Edward Elgar &
Barrington Pheloung

CELLO CONCERTO

1st movement (Adagio, Moderato)

Edward Elgar
Arranged by the composer
for cello and piano

THE HOLIDAY SONG

Based on a theme by Bernard Fleiss

Barrington Pheloung

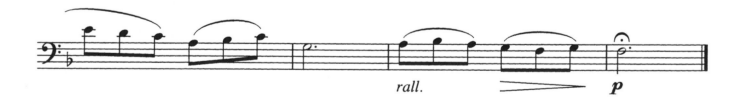

THE FARMHOUSE

Barrington Pheloung

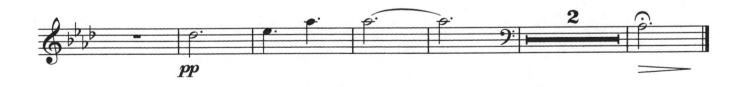

SISTERS

Barrington Pheloung

A DAY ON A BEACH

Barrington Pheloung

CELLO CONCERTO

3rd movement (Adagio)

Edward Elgar
Arranged by the composer
for cello and piano

ROMANCE
Op.62

Edward Elgar

Bowed and fingered by
Julian Lloyd Webber

11

CONTENTS

Order No. NOV120857
ISBN 0-85360-960-8

This book © Copyright 1999 Novello & Company Limited.
14–15 Berners Street, London W1T 3LJ

A DAY ON A BEACH

Barrington Pheloung

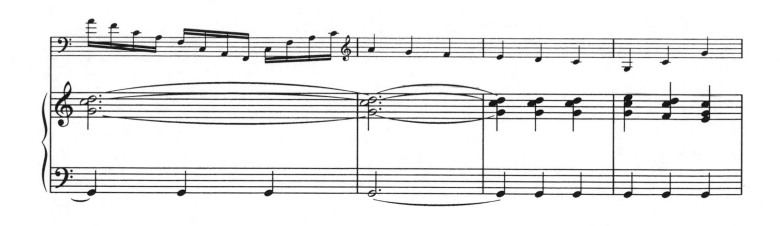

cresc. al fine

cresc. al fine

18

CELLO CONCERTO

3rd movement (Adagio)

Edward Elgar
Arranged by the composer
for cello and piano

ROMANCE
Op.62

Edward Elgar

23

25